Second Wind

2003-2004 NMI
MISSION EDUCATION RESOURCES

❊ ❊ ❊

READING BOOKS

THE FAR SIDE OF THE SEA
From the Philippines to Ukraine
by Lynn DiDominicis

FLOODS OF COMPASSION*
Hope for Honduras
by Paul Jetter

IMPACT!*
Work and Witness Miracles
by J. Wesley Eby

THE JAGGED EDGE OF SOMEWHERE*
by Amy Crofford

THE LAND OF THE LONG WHITE CLOUD
Nazarenes in New Zealand
by Connie Griffith Patrick

SECOND WIND
Running the Race in Retirement
by Sherry Pinson

*Youth Books

❊ ❊ ❊

ADULT MISSION EDUCATION RESOURCE BOOK

CALLED TO GO
Edited by Wes Eby

Second Wind

Running the Race in Retirement

by
Sherry Pinson

Nazarene Publishing House
Kansas City, Missouri

Copyright 2003
by Nazarene Publishing House

ISBN 083-412-0178

Printed in the United States of America

Editor: J. Wesley Eby
Cover Design: Michael Walsh

10 9 8 7 6 5 4 3 2 1

Dedication

For Deanne

Sherry Pinson came to the Church of the Nazarene in 1989. A member of Springdale Church of the Nazarene in Cincinnati, Ohio, she has taught an adult women's Sunday School class, has served on the church board, and sings with the choir. She also produces a monthly newsletter for her church's Nazarene Missions International (NMI) council and was a member of a Work and Witness team that traveled to Hazard, Kentucky, the trip that prompted this book.

Among Sherry's treasures is her involvement with the CIS (Commonwealth of Independent States) Partnership, a group of laypersons who support the work of Nazarene missionaries on the CIS Field.

A freelance writer and editor, Sherry works with Nazarene Communications Network (NCN) News and is a regular columnist and occasional contributing author for *Holiness Today.*

Contents

Eastern Kentucky

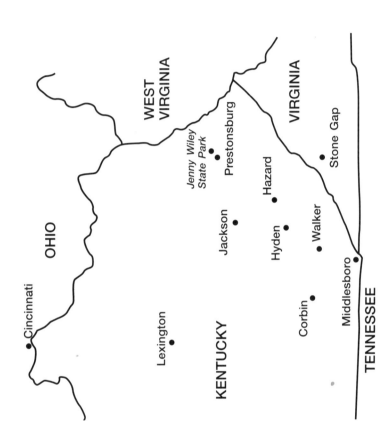

PART 1
Good Work in Appalachia

Gaylan and Sandy Good

Gaylan and Sandy Good

1
Solomon's Temple

The feet of the Appalachian Mountains still lie tucked under a blanket of early morning fog when Gaylan and Sandy Good start their Sundays. The way to church isn't far—Hazard, Kentucky, isn't that big—but the Goods' route takes them miles out of their way, up steep mountain tracks and down hidden "hollers." Along the way they find their congregation, each small member waiting for a ride to Good Shepherd Church of the Nazarene. A stop here, a honk there, and before long the donated van and the Goods' own car are brimming with lively children, the heart and happy soul of the church.

Gaylan and Sandy are pastors of Good Shepherd Nazarene. The church sits in a grass-and-gravel crescent just past the railroad tracks. Big trees throw welcome shade over the rear of the property just before it tumbles down a steep bank to a hidden street below.

Two modular buildings, small and not new, sit perpendicular to one another. One houses the sanctuary and classrooms. Inside, paneling covers the walls. Pine altars grace the front of the sanctuary, and their warm finish reflects light from the windows down each side. Sturdy blue fabric cushions two rows of pews, enough seating for about 65 people. Down the center aisle and beyond the hallway rest room are two truly child-sized classrooms, one on either side.

The second building houses the Master's Lambs Ministry. A tiny galley kitchen across one end opens up into the main meeting room. Closets down the hallway hold supplies for compassionate ministry, and an office runs across the other end. More ministry supplies line its walls, leaving just enough room to get to the desk and roll the wooden chair around a bit.

It's a temple every bit as splendid as Solomon's.

[·] Solomon's Temple in Hazard

2
Culture Shock

Splendid isn't the first word you'd use for Hazard, a small city huddled in the Appalachian Mountains in southeastern Kentucky. The main road curves along the narrow valley floor, hugging the North Fork of the Kentucky River. Some of the shops on Main Street have their faces right on the sidewalk and their backs tight against the mountain. Streets lined with tidy 1920s bungalows climb away from the river. Outside town, paved roads climb through switchbacks, passing scattered houses that would fit in any affluent suburb. Other switchbacks, graveled or dirt, lead to shabby houses hidden in the forest. You can't go far in Hazard without running into forests or mountains.

Hazard was established in 1824 as a post office and county seat for Perry County, but after 88 years only 537 people lived there. An impassable ocean of mountains climbed around the tiny settlement in all directions. Supplies had to come by boat from Jackson, 45 miles downstream, or from Stone Gap, Virginia, in wagons dragged by mules over Big Black Mountain, a two- or three-week trip.[1] Hazard was hard to get into and hard to get out of, so for nearly a century it was just a trading post for families making do on "scratch" farms hidden among the mountains.

Everything—*everything*—changed in 1912.

Blasting through solid rock and bridging tumbling streams, the L & N Railroad laid track through Hazard, and the coal industry rolled its industrialized juggernaut into eastern Kentucky. Hazard folks had dug coal for years, mostly for local use. But with the coming of the railroad and coal companies, thousands and thousands of tons of the glistening mineral were wrested out of the mountains. Hazard's population exploded to more than 4,000 in just eight years and almost doubled in the next decade.[2]

The unskilled mountain laborers... belonged to the company.

Understanding the ministry of Gaylan and Sandy Good isn't possible without understanding what big coal did to eastern Kentucky. Before, families lived isolated from one another, separated by streams and ridges. Afterward, they crowded together in company towns. Before, they lived by subsistence farming, a little trading, and hunting. Afterward, men who had rarely handled cash suddenly earned wages and shopped at company stores. Before, they shared a common background and culture as descendants of western Europeans. Afterward, eastern European immigrants and the African-Americans who built the railroad poured into the area to feed mining's insatiable appetite for labor. Suddenly the mountain people were surrounded by cultures and languages they'd never heard before. The unskilled mountain laborers rented company houses, paid company-set prices at company stores, sent their children to company schools, and saw company doctors when they were sick. They belonged to the company.[3]

But things were booming! Hazard had a new water plant, a sewer system, and—finally!—paved streets. World War I closed down European mines and pushed the price of Kentucky coal way up. People who had lived in poverty for generations now lived in a vigorous town with money in their pockets.

Mostly unaware of the treasure beneath their feet, mountain families often sold the mineral rights to their land to businessmen and speculators, who left them the right to farm—and the burden of taxes. The coal industry was indeed booming, but coal money, piled high in rail cars, flowed right out of the mountains and into the pockets of investors.

Not even war lasts forever. By the early 1920s,

Hazard, Kentucky, in the heart of Appalachia

demand for Kentucky coal had faltered. Fewer and fewer dollars maintained the company houses, stores, and schools. Fewer and fewer dollars ensured safety in the mines. Then came the 1929 stock market crash. Failing coal companies closed the mines and abandoned the towns they had built. Federal aid stepped in, and by 1933 nearly every family in some eastern Kentucky counties was on the dole.[4]

President Franklin Roosevelt's New Deal did bring work to the region, but paychecks still depended on the government. For many families, the New Deal merely cemented a fundamental shift in perspective born in company towns years before: their sturdy independence crumbled under overwhelming need, and government help was accepted, welcomed, and finally expected.

World War II boosted demand for coal, but by then the industry employed machines instead of miners. Coal production continued to boom off and on, but coal employment didn't and never would again. Thousands of mountain workers headed north to factories in Cincinnati, Detroit, and other cities. Between 1940 and 1960, some eastern Kentucky counties lost half or more of their populations.[5] Young people and the better educated simply left. Most who remained behind sank into poverty and weary dependence.

The region's desperation caught the nation's heart. President Lyndon Johnson launched the War on Poverty in the mid-1960s. In Hazard, a community college opened in 1968, and in the early 1990s, a fine hospital.

Drawn by the beauty of the mountains, tourists come in ever-growing numbers to some counties, and Perry County aggressively courts new industries. The stubborn unemployment rate is finally falling, although still higher than the national average. High school graduation rates are up. But despite these advances, 32 percent of the people in Perry County still struggle below the poverty line, more than twice the national average.[6]

It is here, to the people trapped in these numbers, this history, and this continuing struggle, that Gaylan and Sandy Good dare to bring the gospel of Jesus Christ.

NOTES

1. *Hazard, Kentucky, and Perry County: A Photographic History.* Copyright 1998, 2002. HazardKentucky.com web site. <www.haznet.tierranet.com/special/history.htm>.

2. HazardKentucky.com web site.

3. Lowell H. Harrison and James C. Klotter, *A New History of Kentucky* (Lexington: The University Press of Kentucky, 1997), 307-8.

4. Harrison, 361.

5. Harrison, 410.

6. "Poverty Rates in Appalachian Kentucky 1990." Updated 1998. Appalachian Regional Commission web site. <www.arc.gov/research/poverty/povky.htm>.

3
Sandy's Promise

Theda Michelle Colwell started out every day at Vacation Bible School (VBS) in a clean Sunday dress. Although her blond curls wandered off in every direction, her chubby face shone every morning from a good scrubbing. But Theda spent VBS getting into everything, and by the end of the morning her little face and once-tidy dress showed the unmistakable effects of her happy exploration. She was only two years old that year, and the Work and Witness team that came to Good Shepherd to lead VBS assigned one worker the sole task of keeping up with Theda.

For Sandy Good, this little girl is the promise of God. Sandy loves children—in fact, she's a pediatric nurse—but she has no children of her own. She was 42 years old when she married Gaylan in November 1989, older than most first-time brides, though certainly not too old to have children. But in a puzzling contradiction with no satisfactory answer except faith, Sandy battled cervical cancer 18 months before her marriage. She won the fight, but at heartbreaking cost; the doctor's weapon was hysterectomy. Even though now married, Sandy would never bear children. A lesser soul might have withered under the scorching injustice. But Sandy is not a lesser soul.

After she and Gaylan married, Sandy entrusted his parents with her questions about what God was doing. Together they sought His promises, and He answered with new light from Isaiah 54:1. "'Sing, O barren woman, you who never bore a child; burst into song, shout for joy, you who were never in labor; because more are the children of the desolate woman than of her who has a husband,' says the LORD."

The new light made no sense at first. How could she possibly have "more children" when she couldn't have any at all? But Sandy and her in-laws, and Gaylan when they shared God's message with him, took the new insight as God's promise for Sandy. Somehow, without question, He would keep it.

Gaylan knew God was prodding him to take early retirement from the J. C. Penney Company, where he'd worked for 32 years. He and Sandy understood that God had new work for them to do. Knowing only that the task would take them to people with no connection to church, they explored possibilities with the World Mission Department of the Church of the Nazarene. They completed cross-cultural training at International Headquarters in Kansas City and expected an overseas assignment as Nazarenes in Volunteer Service (NIVS). They certainly did not expect to venture less than two hours east from their home in Corbin, Kentucky.

God was getting ready to bring Sandy "more children."

But Appalachian Compassionate Ministries was looking to plant a church in Hazard, starting with a compassionate ministry to mothers and children. So to Hazard they went in January 1994. And there, God kept His promise.

The compassionate ministry idea was not fully formed even as the Goods accepted the call to the mountain mission. Nearby Middlesboro already offered hygiene supplies. Back home in Corbin, another ministry supplied clothing. God's Pantry, a Lexington mission that distributes food, had opened a satellite office not far away in Prestonsburg. What was God thinking?

"I don't remember how or when the idea emerged," Sandy recalls, "but Gaylan says at some point I began talking about a 'baby pantry.'" Babies require a lot of stuff—diapers, formula, cribs, high chairs, car seats, and tiny clothes that are quickly outgrown. God was way ahead on the to-do list, and by March 1994 the Goods' basement and garage were stuffed with baby supplies. The Master's Lambs Ministry opened in Hazard that same month in the Goods' home. God was getting ready to bring Sandy "more children."

During their first weeks in Hazard, Sandy visited all the community agencies in Perry County to build a network for referrals to Master's Lambs. As a volunteer with Americorps, she went from house to house to survey mothers. Were they expecting? Did they have other children? Did they receive health care? Did they know about breast-feeding? Somewhere among these visits, Sandy came in contact with Clarence and Gloria Colwell.

Their story is too familiar to the Goods. In his early 30s, Clarence is good-looking and rail-thin. His worn jeans barely hang on his hips. A gifted mechanic, Clarence can take apart an engine and convince it to run again, but he drifts from job to job without purpose and is unemployed most of the time. He has moved his family from one government-subsidized apartment to another. When they can't make the rent, they move in with Gloria's mother. When the Goods first met the Colwells, Clarence and Gloria had two young daughters and lived on "the draw"—government checks. A third baby was on the way.

Master's Lambs had helped other mothers and children before the Colwells came, but Gloria was the first woman who was pregnant when she first came to the ministry for help. Gloria is a short, stocky woman, not too heavy but squarely built. Her dark hair hangs to her shoulders. Like many of the women from the mountains, she is timid with strangers. Sandy gently put her at ease and then guided her through prenatal care, helping her understand her new baby's health depended on the care she gave herself.

Gaylan and Sandy opened not just the baby pantry to the young family but their hearts as well. Before long, Gloria offered to help in the pantry, sorting donations and helping keep track of who received diapers and who needed formula. Clarence warmed to Gaylan and eventually took to calling him "Daddy." "I can't leave without my hug, Daddy," he will say after helping Gaylan with an odd job. A tender bond has grown between the two very different men, one centered in God's will and sparkling with energy, the other adrift in a culture that offers little hope to its young men.

Theda with her mother, Gloria *(right)*, and Sandy Good

The Goods see promise in Clarence and Gloria that the couple cannot yet see themselves. But for Sandy, one promise already has been wondrously, joyously kept. On December 1, 1994, Theda Michelle Colwell was born. She is the first of Sandy's "more children," a delightful and busy little girl who counts a day lost if there isn't some adventure in it. Although Clarence and Gloria aren't comfortable going to church despite their love for Gaylan and Sandy, Theda knows no such shyness. She's ready when the van comes to wherever her family is living, and sometime during every service, she'll make her way to Sandy and snuggle up against her. For five-year-old Theda, God's love travels in a straight line. Sandy says Jesus loves her. And so, of course, He does.

4
From Penney's to Hazard

Raised in a Mennonite home, Gaylan Good was 12 years old when he first met the Lord. Though the two weren't always walking the same direction during Gaylan's early teen years, it wasn't long before God made sure Gaylan understood His promise of eternal life. Gaylan says, "I began to think about my actions or decisions in the light of 'What would Jesus do?' I found that my actions spoke louder than my words and that people would see as well as hear that I was a Christian. I started teaching Sunday School at 17, and the Lord blessed me with more than 30 years of helping others through Sunday School and Vacation Bible School."

It was a settled, Nazarene sort of life. Gaylan and his wife, Joyce, had four children from 1960 to 1967, and the Goods trusted that if they were faithful to God, active in their church, and careful to live out their faith at home, the children would thrive. Gaylan worked for the J. C. Penney Company in Chattanooga, Tennessee, and Atlanta before earning a promotion to store manager, first in Marietta, Georgia, and then in Athens, 70 miles east. He considered God his business partner, and together they were successful; the stores Gaylan managed showed sales gains when other stores did not.

In Chattanooga Gaylan and Joyce discovered the Church of the Nazarene. "There was no Mennonite church in that city, and the Nazarenes found us and loved us in," says Gaylan. The Goods happily busied themselves with their work, children, and church. Although Joyce had been diagnosed with diabetes in 1962 during her second pregnancy, the disease was carefully monitored and controlled, and it seemed that life would continue its satisfying routine.

But in 1982 the disease abandoned its furtive battle plan and attacked full on, striking first with a diabetic coma. For the next six and a half years, Joyce struggled against its inexorable siege, enduring heart disease, kidney problems, and diabetic neuropathy, eventually losing her vision as well as control of her lower trunk. "During this time, we learned a much deeper trust in God," says Gaylan, "especially the value of prayer. We learned to feel the support of Christian friends and knew we weren't alone in the journey. Without God's strength and power, we probably would have failed."

It was during Joyce's illness that the call to missions came to Gaylan. He already had been thinking of early retirement to pursue a different career, something less demanding. In 1982 news of a Work and Witness trip to Venezuela caught his attention, but with Joyce so ill, he couldn't go. Then, in the spring of 1987, an opportunity came to join a Work and Witness team to the Azores. Joyce's health had stabilized enough for Gaylan to travel, and after the trip he began to think that God might use him in missions or some other church-related work after retirement. Still, he couldn't see how that could work; Joyce's health was just too fragile for him to commit the time and energy such work would require.

In the fall of 1987, Joyce's health suddenly worsened, and a downturn in the stock market threatened J. C. Penney and Gaylan's job. He remembers it as an unsettled time: "In spite of all that God had done for us, I was trying to control my life, my job, my destiny. I was looking to move to a different Penney's store and watched as two manager positions came open in Tennessee. In each case, the door closed. Another position opened up in Virginia. Again, God said no.

"I was focused on such things as the 'right home' for a manager-executive and my involvement in civic and government activities. Yes, I was still active in the church, but I was trying to be self-dependent. I figured God needed my expertise to figure things out. Like King Agrippa in Acts 26, I was in the 'almost' zone. I couldn't really identify the last band of bondage, but I knew I was only 'almost' happy.

"True happiness lies in holiness and the abundant life only Christ can give, and I came to that realization one evening in November 1987. I cried out to God, and He whispered, 'Just take your hands off and let Me be in control.' That night I gave it all back to God, and life has not been the same since."

Within four months, God had opened unmistakable doors for Gaylan to manage the Penney's store in Corbin, Kentucky. There he and Joyce found

> *"I thought one of them looked like an angel,"* Gaylan says. *"I adjusted my trifocals and saw that it was Sandy."*

a home, a larger church family that warmly welcomed them, and a work situation so good that Gaylan calls the last 5½ years of his career the most rewarding of all his 32 years in business.

About a year after Gaylan's encounter with God, Joyce began to lose her battle. She was on dialysis four days a week and by December 1988 had slipped into a coma. She died in February 1989, just 49 years old.

Some time after Joyce's death, the church held revival services. From his vantage point in the choir loft, Gaylan saw two women coming down the aisle. "I thought one of them looked like an angel," he says. "I adjusted my trifocals and saw that it was Sandy.

"In one of the other services, all people under age 42 were asked to stand, and Sandy stood up. Then I knew she was an angel under 42!

"Not long afterward, Sandy joined the Tuesday morning prayer meeting, which was followed by lunch. Somehow, the empty seat was always across from or next to her. Then she and her friends joined my group for a sandwich after Sunday evening services, and—what a coincidence—the empty seat again was always next to Sandy. God and our friends were ganging up on me!"

At both camp meeting and district assembly that year, others mistook them for husband and wife. Finally, Gaylan had to know what Sandy was thinking.

"I asked Sandy to talk with me when we got back to Corbin after the assembly. I needed to know some things, I told her. When we parted, we agreed to pray for God's clear direction. We had such joy and peace that we were each inspired to write the other a letter expressing our feelings. My daddy married us in November 1989. And I'm here to tell you that the heart beats and pounds at age 51 just as it does at 21!"

5
Sandy's Call

A missionary to Saudi Arabia visited a youth camp in 1957, and 12-year-old Sandy Blaney of Kittanning, Pennsylvania, heard God call her to the mission field too. He made the call even clearer when she was 16 and her youth group toured missions in Appalachia. "I asked God to help me return to this region to serve," Sandy recalls. "As a high school senior, I applied to one school of nursing, the best in our area. With the innocence of youth, I promised God if He would help me get accepted, I'd never ask Him for anything ever again. God answered that prayer, but I have to admit I've asked Him for a lot of things since then!"

Although Sandy's dad didn't go to church, her mother took Sandy and her sister to a Presbyterian church, where Sandy was confirmed and received her First Communion. But the faith and call to missions that had seemed so clear at age 16 dimmed and faltered as she sought first a bachelor of science degree and then a master's degree in pediatric nursing. Under the strain of her studies, full-time job, and what Sandy calls her "liberal" lifestyle, she drifted away from her call. "I knew my life was out of God's will," she says, "but I rationalized by promising Him that if He just got me through school, then I would do something for Him.

"The crisis came in 1977 when I realized my life was in pieces. I fell to my knees in my apartment living room and pleaded with the Lord to take control of my life. Not two weeks later, I heard about the Lend-a-Hand Center in Walker, Kentucky, and I joined a group to volunteer one week to screen school-age children.

"I fell asleep on the ride and awakened just as we reached the bridge that leads to Lend-a-Hand. I could see the mission across the valley, and I knew in that instant my life would profoundly change. In 1979, after two more years of graduate study, I returned to Lend-a-Hand as a full-time volunteer."

Sandy could not have known just how profound the change would eventually be. At the mission she met Peggy Kemner, Lend-a-Hand's codirector, who became her friend and mentor. Peggy introduced her to the Church of the Nazarene, and Sandy began attending the Nazarene church in Corbin. As she watched Peggy's life, Sandy was drawn toward a deep desire to commit everything to the Lord. Her Presbyterian background hadn't prepared her for the Nazarene doctrine of holiness, but Peggy patiently helped her understand it.

One morning, as Sandy was driving through Buckeye Hollow, her van broke down. "I turned to the Lord for wisdom. I believe I reminded Him that I was down in that hollow because I was working in His service. Then He jarred my attitude and understanding by whispering, 'I want all of you.' As soon as I could, I ran to Peggy with this exciting news. He wanted all of me! I had habits that needed to be discarded, attitudes that needed to be changed. I needed to learn what a personal relationship with our risen Lord really means. God's grace, Peggy's patience, and the friendship and love of my church literally lifted me out of rebellion and into the plan that God had for me." In December 1979, Sandy asked Jesus to be her Savior.

Sandy and Gaylan were ordained together as elders in the Church of the Nazarene.

"I gave up smoking," Sandy recalls. "When I had gone a year without a cigarette, I asked to be baptized and was immersed in 1980 on my 33rd birthday." But by early 1981, it was clear to Sandy that she could not, even by her very best efforts, live as God intended. "I was beginning to learn that until my will was aligned with God's, He surely wouldn't have all of me, nor would I be of use in His service. On Pentecost Sunday in 1981, I carried my 'unknown bundle' to the altar and was sanctified. God patiently taught me to bring my strong-willed personality under His control. Finally I was able to say, 'Now, Lord, You have all of me.'"

Once God possessed all of Sandy, He got busy with His plans for her. Always eager to learn, Sandy began to study for the office of deaconess in the Church of the Nazarene. One evening, during a class about holiness, Sandy sensed a call to preach. She had struggled with the idea for years, but when the teacher said, "Appalachia needs women ministers to interpret holiness for women," her soul was pierced through. At the Eastern Kentucky District Assembly in 1998, Sandy and Gaylan were ordained together as elders in the Church of the Nazarene.

That step, taken together, captures the essence of Gaylan and Sandy's marriage. The call to Hazard came to both of them, and together they see themselves as servants who go where the Master wants to send them. Sandy describes the place of peace where she finds herself today: "Gaylan and I are happy, optimistic people who can rise above obstacles to look at the goal set before us. We rarely experience conflict in our marriage, and God supplies places and times for renewal when we need it most. We work together well, and we have complementary gifts as well as great energy. We both sense we're in the center of God's will, and our lives are enriched because of this assurance."

6

Getting Serious About John 21:15

"Would you, Gaylan and Sandy, be willing to take the assignment?"

Talking with the Goods at the Eastern Kentucky District Assembly in March 1993, the district superintendent fired directly at the heart of the Hazard question. The plan to open a compassionate ministry for moms and babies and the even bigger dream of planting a church couldn't get off the ground without leadership. Would the Goods take on the task?

Gaylan and Sandy were stunned, unable to respond. Yes, they already had offered themselves as Nazarenes in Volunteer Service. And, true, their overseas assignment to Papua New Guinea had fallen through, so that door definitely had closed. But they still expected a similar assignment outside the United States. They were volunteers after all, and they dreamed of serving somewhere with career missionaries. Now the district superintendent had turned their thoughts upside down. Not Papua New Guinea, thousands of miles away, but Hazard, Kentucky, 85 miles to the east. Not assisting career missionaries but actually being the missionaries. Not settling into an established mission but starting from scratch. They could give no immediate answer except the promise to pray.

As God always does, He had laid some plans ahead of time. Months before, Sandy had surprised Gaylan with reservations for a weekend at Jenny Wiley State Park not far from Hazard. Secluded high in the mountains, the park is so popular that guests are allowed to make reservations up to three years in advance. How like God to have arranged a reservation for April 1993, just a few weeks after the Goods promised to pray about the work in Hazard.

"God's timing was perfect," says Sandy. The weekend away gave the Goods a chance to see Hazard as well as some quiet time to discuss the superintendent's question and pray about it. They first saw Hazard as a quaint little town. The business area was still lively. Houses were well-maintained, and residents had planted flowers and shrubs. "But after living in Appalachia for many years, we could see the not-so-subtle signs of poverty-stricken people," Sandy explains.

But if God truly wanted Gaylan and Sandy in Hazard, He still had some work to do. As they toured the town, they found few houses for sale. And they didn't need just any house. It had to be large enough to store things for the ministry, easy to find, and modest enough that needy people would be comfortable coming there.

By the end of their getaway weekend, though, the Goods were sure. They accepted the assignment and put their house in Corbin on the market. Gaylan retired in September at the age of 55, and that same month their house sold. They were ready for Hazard, but Hazard still wasn't ready for them. They simply could not find a suitable house.

"It came to me during the night to check on an old house," Gaylan says. So they went back for a second look at a house they had already checked off their list, a real "fixer-upper." The "For Sale" sign was gone! They were too late. At a loss, they walked next door to see if the neighbor knew anything about the status of the house. Yes, it was sold, but wasn't it odd? She wanted to sell her house too! She had prayed that God would send a buyer when the time was right. Now here were the Goods, right at her doorstep.

In just a couple of months, the Master's Lambs Ministry pantry was fully stocked and ready to open.

Neither Gaylan nor Sandy was impressed with the house from the outside. Sandy wondered whether it would even be worth coming back the next day to see it. Nevertheless, back they went, and God showed them what they did not see on their own. Walking from room to room, Sandy began to see exactly how the house could fit the ministry. Even the price was right. After more prayer they were convinced, and the Church of the Nazarene came to Hazard in the form of a compassionate ministry to new mothers and babies at 426 Mulberry Street.

As Gaylan and Sandy settled into the house in January 1994, God's advance work became even more apparent. In 1993 a Work and Witness team from Michigan had gathered baby-care things, loaded up a truck, and delivered the items to Mercy Mission in Middlesboro. There they had sat, waiting for the Goods. Once settled in Hazard, Gaylan got another call from Middlesboro. A 15-foot truck from New Jersey had arrived loaded with clothing, diapers, a few high chairs, and other baby furnishings. Then a 24-foot truck sent by World Vision unexpectedly showed up at the Mulberry Street house. By then the basement was full, so Gaylan and Sandy crammed the truckload of diapers, coats, and more than 70 car seats into their garage. The Goods started speaking at churches throughout the Eastern Kentucky District, and invariably each church would hold a baby shower for the mission. In just a couple of months, the Master's Lambs Ministry pantry was fully stocked and ready to open.

The first young mother to visit the baby pantry came in March 1994 to ask for a box of diapers. Sandy welcomed her into the living room of their home. From that small start, the ministry served about 100 families a month through the rest of 1994. Of those, 85 percent were unemployed or disabled. And overwhelmingly, heartbreakingly, they were young; 30 percent were 13 to 19 years old and 49 percent were 20 to 25. Forty-four percent of the women were divorced or had never married. All were receiving government assistance of some kind. Through 1995, more than 200 families came to

Mulberry Street for help every month, and the ministry took over most of Goods' basement and all of their living room. God's promise to Sandy was coming true day by day as the ministry served pregnant women and those with children three years of age or younger.

The goal of the baby pantry is to ensure these vulnerable little ones have what they need—nutritional support and proper clothing, as well as equipment to keep them safe. But their moms find more

The "lambs" in their first Christmas program

at the baby pantry than what is stacked on the shelves. For many, being cared for is a new experience. And as they learn to care for their babies, they also learn how important their influence is—how important they really are in the lives of their children. Grateful for the help and with a new sense of their value, several have volunteered to help at the pantry. Two of the mothers eventually came to serve on the ministry's board of directors.

In 2000, the Mennonite Central Committee offered to help the Goods advertise for someone to oversee the pantry full-time, and Darby Kilmer took on the task in September of that year. In 2001, 494 families came to the baby pantry for help in 3,092 visits, an average of 60 per week. Hidden in those numbers are 659 children touched by the love of God through the Master's Lambs Ministry.

Where children are concerned, Sandy isn't content just to wait for needy mothers to find her. She goes out looking. As the pantry ministry grew, God opened another door. The director of Appalachian Compassionate Ministries in Middlesboro heard about a new program that seemed tailor-made for Sandy's gifts and skills. Through Vanderbilt University, Americorps and Volunteers in Service to America (VISTA) wanted to establish Maternal Infant Health Outreach Worker (MIHOW) programs in eastern Kentucky. The program would train Sandy to recruit and train other women from Perry County to mentor expectant mothers. Instead of waiting for women to find the baby pantry on their own, Sandy and Gaylan would have a way to reach children before they were born. With good prenatal care, "Sandy's children" would have an even better chance at a good start.

A year passed before Sandy could find qualified women who met MIHOW's criteria and were willing to commit to the required 60 hours of training and the demands of mentoring. First to come was a woman whose daughter-in-law found help at the pantry. A second woman came to help after Gaylan and Sandy spoke at her Baptist church. A third came after her husband heard the Goods talk about the work at a local Lion's Club meeting. Others joined the effort as well. Eventually the program expanded enough to need a supervisor.

In the summer of 2000, a woman named Emily, a neighbor, came to Gaylan and Sandy for prayer. Her child support was ending, she said, and she needed work. Sandy hired her to clean the church for a month but couldn't offer much beyond that. Then God opened another door for both Emily and the MIHOW program. Though a grant, Sandy was able to hire Emily to supervise the MIHOW home visitors.

MIHOW specifically targets women whose poverty, stress, and isolation put their children at high risk for abuse, neglect, and educational, developmental, and medical problems. Visiting in the women's homes at least once a month, the MIHOW mentors teach the mothers-to-be how healthy children develop and grow, encouraging the moms to work on healthy lifestyles and good parenting skills.

The mentors give more than just practical advice. They also offer a listening ear without judging the young mothers, who have so much to learn in a short time and often find little support for their efforts. According to the program's meticulous records, not one father among the 41 families enrolled in the program in 2001 was actively participating. The commitment of the MIHOW workers is therefore especially critical. These home visitors, who earn just $4,000 per year plus mileage, stick close by the mothers for the first three years of the child's life. One home visitor explains the long view the MIHOW workers take: "The children are an important aspect of my visit. We provide the young mothers with information about pregnancy and what to expect during delivery, along with the stages their children will go through as they grow. . . . Still, I feel that a lot of emphasis should be placed on the mother. If she's well and happy, then she's able to accomplish more for her children."

Month in and month out, MIHOW mentors listen, teach, encourage, intervene—whatever it takes to lift the moms and their children out of a bleak, confining history and turn them toward a healthy, hopeful, wide-open future.

7

God Drives a '63 Cadillac

KIDS in Hazard is where kids usually are—not far from a McDonald's restaurant. KIDS—Kentucky Infant Development Station, Inc.—sits right on Main Street in downtown Hazard, catercorner from the local McDonald's. KIDS is MIHOW headquarters in Perry County. The building's windows look out on the busiest street in town. Its second story includes a small apartment that college and nursing interns can use. KIDS looks like any ordinary commercial building, but in reality it's one more miracle in the story of Gaylan and Sandy's ministry and testimony to God's creative fund-raising.

First came manna out of the blue—or out of the brown. In May 1997 an area supervisor for United Parcel Service (UPS) asked the Goods to submit a grant proposal for a capital expenditure to improve their ministry's services. Gaylan and Sandy had organized the Master's Lamb Ministry baby pantry and the MIHOW program under the KIDS name, and MIHOW in particular needed a home. In the grant proposal, the Goods described their vision for a comprehensive program that could reach out to expectant and new mothers and their children. They described a community-based center that could bring health-care professionals and poor women together. They emphasized the need for materials written for below-average readers, and they wrote of their desire to help young mothers make the most of their limited resources. Persuasive as always when talking about the work God has called them to do, the Goods landed the grant—$25,000.

The person who bought the Cadillac wasn't just a fan of fine old cars; he was the president of a local bank.

Then came more manna from Michigan. A woman called to offer the ministry her father's 1963 Cadillac. He had recently died, and she wanted to settle the estate. If the Goods would give her a receipt for its value, the car would be theirs.

Without seeing the car, Gaylan and Sandy agreed to take it. When it arrived in Hazard, the Goods found themselves in possession of a mint-condition classic. The Cadillac sat just one day under their carport before two men stopped to see it. Three days later the father of the one of those men bought it for $12,000.

But God is the master multiplier. The person who bought the Cadillac wasn't just a fan of fine old cars; he was the president of a local bank. Gaylan

The '63 Cadillac

went to his office to take care of the paperwork for the car and—never shy about God's work—he told the bank president about the UPS grant and their search for a building for KIDS. It just so happened, the president said, that the bank had a building for sale, a former pool hall sitting empty on Main Street near McDonald's. The bank had recently turned down an offer of $50,000 for it, but he could let KIDS have it for that amount. Would Gaylan be interested?

More than merely interested, Gaylan was convinced that God had specifically arranged for KIDS to have that building. His certainty rose even higher when he got a call two weeks later from a church in Cincinnati that wanted to send a small Work and Witness team to Hazard—a team that included a builder and an electrician. Three days after the team's arrival, $12,000 in renovations were finished and paid for. The Kentucky Infant Development Station was ready for business.

8
Pat's People Heart

"She is more of a mother to us than our own mothers," said one couple about MIHOW volunteer Pat Sumner.

Pat, 51, has been a home visitor since 1996 and at one point was mentoring 17 young women. Although diabetes has increasingly damaged her health and now keeps her from taking on new moms when others "graduate," she continues to visit the 6 still under her watchful eye—the ones she worries about most.

Pat first met the Goods at the baby pantry. Her son and pregnant daughter-in-law had hit a rough patch financially and had moved in temporarily with Pat and her husband. Pat describes herself as a "people person," and she and Sandy would talk when Pat came to the pantry for diapers or baby food for her new grandchild. "You seem like such a nice person," Sandy said one day, and she told Pat about the MIHOW program. Pat became Sandy's first volunteer.

A grandma seven times over, Pat knows a thing or two about babies. And she also knows something about the human spirit: people wither under the burning heat of "you should" and "you shouldn't," but they bloom under the soft sunshine of loving guidance. "Sometimes a girl just needs another mom to talk to," she says. "Sometimes she doesn't have a mom around or her mom is controlling."

Pat still volunteers her time even though VISTA now provides grant money for a small stipend. "If I got paid with money," Pat says, "I wouldn't get the pay I get now. Somebody told me I'm working for a reward in heaven, but I said, 'I get my reward right here—smiles and hugs from my girls and their babies.' If you do something from the heart, you work harder."

Pat listens to them and loves them all, one at a time.

Some of the women Pat works with are young and alone in their pregnancies with no father in the picture. Others are married but face financial problems that overwhelm their already strained resources. Some deal with perplexing problems of their own making. Some struggle with problems dumped on them by others. Pat listens to them and loves them all, one at a time.

"I don't judge anybody," Pat continues. "I don't put anybody down. The girls tell me their secrets, but I never look shocked. I'm not perfect myself, and I don't know anybody who is. God created all of us, and we're all just a soul inside a body. So I never think or say, 'Look how bad you are,' and I don't tell them what to do. Instead, I ask questions. 'Is this the best thing for you and your baby?' I might ask. The questions lead them to make their own decisions about what's best. And when they make a decision, they hear it in their own voice, not me telling them what to do."

One shy, young woman thought so little of herself that she often wasn't clean, and others had noticed it. Pat might have given her a lecture or a list of hygiene rules. Instead, she waited and watched, and one day she noticed the girl had done something different with her hair. It still wasn't clean, but Pat ignored that. "I like what you did with your hair," she said. "It looks pretty that way." At the next visit, the young woman's hair was washed and shining. A tiny step, to be sure, but one tiny step followed another, and now that young mother is working in a shop downtown and taking care of her own needs.

A more difficult situation involved a woman who was trying to balance two men in her life. One man seemed to connect with one of her children, while the other seemed to care about another child. Eventually, as she thought about Pat's questions and identified her own strengths, she decided to step away from both men until she was sure of what she really needed. She made new friends and learned that she didn't have to push her own needs aside to please someone into caring about her.

Pat tells about another young woman: "I talked with her about reading to her baby, how important it is. 'But I can't read,' she said. I told her she still could look at picture books or coloring books with her baby.

"Next time I saw her, she showed me what she'd done. She couldn't afford to buy books, so she had drawn pictures and written a story the best she could spell and put the pages together in a little book. It didn't matter if the words were spelled wrong. She knew what she meant. And that baby would look up at her mom with a big smile and wide eyes when she read the story to her. That mom really loves her baby, and she really wants to read to her. I think she will learn to read along with her daughter when the girl starts school.

"I visit my clients once a month or more often if they need it, but they can call me anytime," Pat says. "Somebody told me I'm a 'half-full' type of person. I think if you help one person—just one person, even with a smile—then, you've helped. I guess I have a people heart."

9
A 20-Year Vision

The baby pantry, home visits, and classes at the KIDS building are only part of the reason God brought Gaylan and Sandy to Hazard. He also sent them to plant a Church of the Nazarene. They looked for space to rent, but their budget could not stretch far enough.

In 1995, a year after the pantry opened, Gaylan heard on the radio about a church for sale. Seating only 65 people, three other congregations had outgrown it, but it would be perfect for a brand-new church. And it sat right across from the county vocational school, a local landmark that everyone in town could find. The owners were selling it fully furnished with pews, carpeting, and even a sound system. The Goods were convinced to buy it when they saw the plaque over the entrance to the main aisle—"Holiness Unto the Lord." Obviously this modular building was meant to be a Nazarene church!

The $10,000 price was doable, and immediately the mother church in Corbin pledged $1,000 and launched a fund-raising campaign. The Eastern Kentucky District sent $5,000; the money had been tucked away in an account specifically for a church plant in Hazard, but, oddly, no one could remember its source. The District Advisory Board promised to cover any shortfall. Another generous donation allowed the Goods to buy a second modular building, which was moved to the church site to house the baby pantry.

Hazard finally had a Church of the Nazarene. Gaylan and Sandy named it Good Shepherd to complement the Master's Lambs Ministry.

The mysterious $5,000 wasn't a mystery at all but a legacy of one man's faithfulness.

Good Shepherd had been a long time coming. Its story started long before Gaylan considered retirement, long before Sandy committed her life fully to God, long before God called them to Hazard. That mysterious $5,000 wasn't a mystery at all but a legacy of one man's faithfulness. His story, carefully detailed in a sheaf of handwritten letters, was finally recovered from a dusty file in the district office.

In August 1970, Andy Pederson boarded a Greyhound bus in Erie, Pennsylvania, and headed for a vacation in Hazard. His aunt Dorothy had been a missionary to the area in the early 1930s. She had been hit by a train as she tried to pull a little girl out of its path on a trestle; both later died at the hospital. Andy talked to several people in the area who remembered his aunt, and as he traveled through the mountains where she had worked, he began to nurture a dream for a Church of the Nazarene in Hazard. Andy began to save a little money from his grocery store job, convinced that the savings could be used to start a church in his aunt's memory. It was a vision he kept intact almost single-handedly for nearly the next 20 years.

For the next two decades, Andy boarded the bus almost every summer to vacation in Hazard; only illness stopped him from coming. And each summer he used his vacation to pass out tracts—632,000, to be exact, according to his meticulous records.

Between visits he wrote letters to the Eastern Kentucky District office, prodding the superintendent to plant a church in Hazard. His last letter was dated June 1988, not long before he died of cancer. The closing lines of that letter read, "I'm still giving out thousands of tracts! *I got lots of fight in me yet.*"

In 1990 the district office received a check for $5,000, identified in a letter from an attorney as the district's "legacy under the will of Andrew A. Pederson, deceased." That $5,000, saved bit by bit from Andy's grocery store wages, helped buy the building that became Good Shepherd Church. Andy's dream, planted 26 years earlier by the memory of his missionary aunt, finally blossomed under the obedient care of Gaylan and Sandy Good.

10

Miss Annie

Miss Annie is 80-something years old now and great-grandmother to five of Good Shepherd's children. A woman used to doing and going, she has been slowed by arthritis in recent years and walks with a cane, "if she's behaving herself," as Sandy says. Annie joined the Church of the Nazarene on Easter of 2000. Her light brown hair bobs in curly ringlets and her eyes twinkle as she shouts her praises to God like an old-time saint.

But under her sweet smile lies a faith of sturdy steel that works hard for others. At her request, Good Shepherd holds Sunday evening services at 6:30 instead of 6:00, because Annie invited her son's friend Raymond to church, and Raymond can't make it until after work. So 6:30 it is. Literally as excited as a child at Christmas, she made sure the church had enough money to decorate for Jesus' birthday. Though she can't read, Annie never misses a missionary reading book on audiotape, and she never misses a chance to give her vibrant testimony of God's faithfulness to her and her family.

Miss Annie has needed His faithfulness. One granddaughter, lost in the desolate abyss of drug abuse, is in and out of jail, and her children, Brandon and Amber, cannot count on her care. They live with their grandmother and grandfather, Dorothy and

Brandon with his mother and grandparents,
Ernest and Dorothy

Ernest, Annie's daughter and son-in-law. Dorothy is
blind, and Ernest has heart trouble, but the children
need them, so they do the best they can. It does seem
that sin sends a taproot down deep in one place and
then creeps like crabgrass in all directions.

But Annie's faith is fighting back in Brandon
and Amber. Brandon's quick intelligence took him
all the way to the regional team when Good Shepherd fielded its first-ever children's quiz team. He is
blossoming as he learns to believe that God does
have a plan for him, that He does see one young boy
tucked away in a tiny church in the Appalachian
Mountains. Now in his midteens, Brandon is quiet,

Miss Annie, next to Pastor Good *(right)*,
along with Richard and Deb

bordering on shy, a deep thinker. Sandy identifies him as the most spiritually mature student in her Sunday School class. A compassionate young man, he has his eye on college and a career as a doctor.

Amber also comes each week to Sunday School, where she finds love and possibility in Sandy's open arms, Gaylan's godly discipline, and Annie's happy faith. Three others of Annie's great-grandchildren join Brandon and Amber, and the five represent hope and a future for a family that has had far too little promise of either one.

11

Safety in Hazard

In an article for the fall 1995 issue of *Grow*, a church growth magazine, Sandy identified the obstacles faced by Good Shepherd. Not long before the church opened, Sandy wrote, "Merely scheduling traditional services probably will not work because the majority of these unchurched people are simply not ready for such an experience. Bound by drinking, drug abuse, poverty, the welfare system, limited transportation . . . [and] generalized apathy and guilt, they will be difficult to reach on a spiritual level. Prayer, patience, persistence, and agape love will loosen their bonds. But we've got to reach beyond the social problems directly into their hearts so we can help with spiritual solutions."

Difficult it proved to be, but God could see a way. After six months of trying unsuccessfully to hold regular services, Good Shepherd invited a group called Kingdom Kompany to hold Vacation Bible School. Most of the children who came either lived in area housing projects or were from families who had been helped by the baby pantry. During that week, God spoke to Sandy and Gaylan. "Focus on the children," He told them.

At the end of VBS, the Goods invited the children back for Sunday morning. Now they drive through the area every Sunday to pick them up.

They send the children to Nazarene summer camp and sponsor a children's quiz team. The kids bring their pennies, nickels, and dimes for Alabaster offerings, and they learn what God can do through them. And little by little, drawn by the church's demonstrated love for their children, some mothers, a few fathers, and some grandparents now attend as well.

Although adults are beginning to come to church, Sandy sees children not as a drawing card but as worthwhile in themselves and the fulfillment of God's promise. She worries like a mother over each one. She wonders if 12-year-old Joshua will learn to control his impulsive behavior and become a minister, as he sincerely wants to do. Drugs have wrecked his parents' lives, and the church is his best hope for stability and purpose. She watches over Desiree, another of Annie's great-grandchildren. Desiree is biracial, not yet a teenager, and lives with her grandmother. Mature beyond her years, the girl already displays profound potential for leadership. And Sandy worries over Mary, 14, who once talked about college but now only hurries home after school to watch her baby brother—the youngest of her siblings, one of several by different fathers.

The doctrine of holiness is even more foreign to them than it was to me.

"There is something undaunted in the kids," Sandy says, "some resilience that keeps them hopeful in spite of the instability that marks their homes." She prays for them all, asking God to keep them from the apathy that binds their parents in drug abuse, damaging relationships, crippling dependence, and spiritual starvation.

"Our congregation is a wonderful mix of the kinds of people Jesus was drawn to in His ministry," says Sandy. "Nearly all the adults are living lives embedded in sin; most of the children come from dysfunctional homes. We have black and white and mixed races, people who wouldn't be welcome in the larger mainline denominations in our community. These folk lack discipline and social graces, yet we love them like family, and somehow this love is binding us into a fellowship. The doctrine of holiness is even more foreign to them than it was to me, but we can see some slowly beginning to change. We long for them to come to salvation and sanctification, so that they may be set free from the bonds of sin."

A year after the church opened, Debra, a Nazarene from Alabama, moved to Hazard and volunteered to teach the younger children in Sunday School while Sandy taught the older kids. Gaylan continued to handle the adult class. Later, the MIHOW supervisor, Emily, volunteered to teach the littlest children, splitting Debra's class. Now the Goods have two dependable lay leaders every Sunday. In 2000 Good Shepherd averaged 20 children and 6 adults on Sunday morning.

The church added an evening service in 1997. Gaylan and Sandy do not pick up the children for that service, which is more traditional, but kids are

Pastor Sandy with "her" children

welcome if they bring a parent along. Richard, Debra's husband, is trying to win Miss Annie's son-in-law, Ernest, through the evening service, but it's uphill work. "Religion is a woman thing," say most of the men.

Gaylan puts his finger on the vague disinterest that permeates the culture among the adults. "We have not experienced any outright resistance," he says. "There's just a pervasive lack of interest in spiritual things. Many are second- and third-generation nonchurch people, and they say, 'Why worry? I'm going to be OK. Maybe before I die I'll do something about religion.' There's very much a live-for-today attitude."

Acting as servants in that environment has required a strong and steady commitment from Gaylan and Sandy, both to the Lord and to each other. Children have few if any resources of their own and could never support a pastor financially, so the Goods have served as volunteers from the beginning of their ministry in Hazard. Gaylan had his retirement from J. C. Penney, but when the stock fell 80 percent in 1999—2000, that income dried up. He took a part-time job with a telephone answering system to help make ends meet. Then in June 2000 his volunteer work with United Way opened the door for him to become executive director, a paid position with no fixed hours. That helped both the Goods and United Way, which saw its income across its eight-county area double the year Gaylan took over.

In the meantime, Sandy returned to school to upgrade her master's degree with a certificate in public health nursing. She studied on-site in Hazard through a satellite-based program out of the University of Kentucky. The intense study and research, piled on top of her duties with MIHOW, the baby pantry, and the church, demanded an extra measure of grace. Both Gaylan and Sandy celebrated when she graduated in May 2001.

Again God used one blessing to spur another. For her research project, Sandy focused on cervical cancer, and through her studies she met one of the coordinators of Kentucky's cancer program. When a similar position opened up in Hyden, about 20 minutes from Hazard, the coordinator remembered Sandy. Though past the deadline for sending a résumé, Sandy faxed hers over and landed an interview. One of the interviewers was a former colleague of Sandy's who knew the quality of her commitment and work, and Sandy got the job—the first full-time paid position in all her years of nursing. But God still wasn't finished multiplying that blessing. The Hyden office of the cancer program moved to Hazard! Sandy's workplace turned out to be in the same building as Gaylan's United Way office.

12
Retired to Serve

Gaylan and Sandy Good have been obedient to God's call, and He has been faithful to honor their commitment to Him and His children. After Gaylan retired, the J. C. Penney Corporation recognized him with the James Cash Penney Retired Associate Award for Volunteer Service. The award gave Gaylan a crystal sculpture to decorate a shelf, but even more important, the honor included $10,000 for him to use in his ministry in Hazard. Sandy was chosen a few years ago to represent VISTA in Washington, D.C., at the volunteer program's 30th anniversary celebration.

The Goods' ministry is growing. They are eager to find more helpers and to help more children and adults come to the Lord. When Gaylan managed stores for Penney's, his duties included mentoring young up-and-comers. Describing the company philosophy, he says, "If you couldn't look back and say, 'I helped this one succeed' and 'I had a hand in that one's success,' then you hadn't done your job." That attitude has stayed with Gaylan. In the first eight years of the work in Hazard, he helped five other compassionate ministry groups from at least three denominations complete their nonprofit paperwork and get off the ground. He hopes for the same sort of multiplying impact among retirees who read this story of their work in Hazard.

Beneath the endless demands on the Goods' time and energy is a bedrock foundation: their love for the Lord and their commitment to one another. Their marriage is strong, a haven for both of them as they together and individually walk through the doors God opens. Sandy particularly rejoices in the fulfillment of God's promise of many children. They look forward to seeing "their" children grow up, perhaps go to college, get married, and then bring up their own children in the new way—the way of purpose and hope—learned from the Lord at Good Shepherd Nazarene.

"Gaylan" and "retire" will never fit comfortably in the same sentence.

Gaylan retired from the business world, but "Gaylan" and "retire" will never fit comfortably in the same sentence. He's busier today than ever, and just as delightfully optimistic and enthusiastic. Now in his mid-60s, his already crackling energy seems only to multiply with the needs God puts before him and Sandy. Clearly, the Goods have gotten their second wind.

Sandy summed up their joy in the article she wrote for *Grow:* "I share this story, not to bring applause for our efforts but to bring prayer and whatever assistance others may wish to offer. Most of all,

I share it to encourage retired laypeople to become involved in service evangelism. Each of us is a steward of our own unique gifts and talents. Step forth in faith and spend them on others, without counting the cost. Love people and respond to God's guidance. He'll do all the rest."

California and Baja California

PART 2

Turning Back at the Border of Retirement

Paul and Tina Jones

Paul and Tina Jones

1
Detour!

Paul and Tina Jones had reached the comfortable stage of life. The hard work of raising children lay behind them; they had brought up their sons, Jerry and Jay, in the church and had seen the boys safely on their way to adulthood. The Joneses had been good stewards of the gifts God had entrusted to them, and they enjoyed a secure income from real estate development. Well respected in their hometown of Montclair, California, they were actively involved in developing the community's strengths. Paul had even served as a Montclair city councilman for 10 years. They had been active, dedicated members of the Church of the Nazarene in Ontario, California, for 20 years, and had been generous with their time and money for the sake of missions.

In 1977 Paul was 55 years old and Tina was 52. There was no particular reason to suspect their future held anything but enjoying the bountiful blessings God had poured out on them.

They weren't aware of it at the time, but all of that began to change the day a traffic accident closed the road through Tijuana, Mexico. Returning from a vacation in Mexico in 1976, the Joneses decided to avoid the traffic congestion and detour through Tecate on the California-Mexico border about 35 miles east of Tijuana. They arrived in

Tecate about noon and stopped for lunch on the California side at Tecate Mission, a small school. A quick stop for a meal stretched into several days; after that they never really left. Oh, it's true that they drove back home to Montclair, but their hearts stayed behind in Tecate.

Tecate Mission takes as its harvest field all the residents of the city—the 230 who live on the United States side and the 67,000 who live on the Mexico side. Several denominations support the mission, which includes an elementary school, church, and small storage building nicknamed the "mouse house" in honor of its many tiny residents. The Joneses' visit stamped the mission on their hearts, and back at Ontario Nazarene they encouraged the congregation to get involved. The church sent food, clothing, and supplies to the mission, and Paul and Tina spent the better part of 10 months there. The people, their needs, and the opportunity for service drove Paul to rededicate his life to the Lord in a way more deeply than he had ever done before.

We feel led to missionary service. We don't know how long— two years, four years, or the rest of our lives.

On November 7, 1977, Paul Jones resigned his seat on the Montclair city council. He and Tina were moving to Tecate permanently, he said, or at least until God told them otherwise. "We really feel a definite call to work at the border crossing," Paul told the council. "We feel led to missionary service. We don't know how long—two years, four years, or the rest of our lives. We must follow God's call.

"I think it's probably difficult for people to understand why someone at age 55 would want to dedicate the rest of his life to Christian service," Paul continued. "I want the opportunity to bring the Good News to others and really get to know God the Creator and how I relate to Him."

God's call did turn out to be open-ended, and He supplied the Joneses with second wind for the task. In March 1978 Paul volunteered to be the mission school's administrator and taught English at Seminario Teólogico de Baja California, a Bible institute just across the border in Mexico. Tina cooked for the children and the staff at Tecate Mission and helped distribute clothing and food from the "mouse house." Once in Tecate, the Joneses never left mission work. Serving first at the mission school, they then developed Vida Nueva (New Life) Compassionate Ministry Center.

A few years ago, after much prayer and meditation, they decided to tell their story. "We want to encourage others in midlife and those contemplating retirement to respond to God's call to advance His kingdom," Paul said. "With good health and long life, we now have an opportunity for ministry at home and around the world. All of us, at every age, can make a difference."

Entrance to Vida Nueva

For Paul and Tina, the responsibility to obey God's call carried even greater weight than simply an opportunity to serve. "The idea of doing nothing but enjoying retirement," Paul said, "brings to mind the sobering words of Galatians 6:9-10: 'Let us not become weary in doing good, for at the proper time we will reap a harvest if we do not give up. Therefore, as we have opportunity, let us do good to all people, especially to those who belong to the family of believers.'"

2

A Strange Visitor

The past month's income and expense statements were spread across Paul Jones's desk in his office at Tecate Mission. Auditing the books wasn't nearly as much fun as watching the children play during recess, but as the administrator Paul was responsible to check the records each month, and he did it carefully. The numbers in their precise columns were a blessing in their own right, because they represented both the mission's benefactors and the children helped each month in Jesus' name.

A shadow interrupted the morning sunshine as it slanted across the desk, and Paul looked up to see a stranger. He was neatly dressed and ordinary looking, but his sudden appearance startled Paul. Without introducing himself, the man said, "Paul Jones, are you looking for a warehouse?"

Taken aback by the abrupt question, Paul answered, "No. Why do you ask?"

"I've been sent to tell you that a warehouse for food, clothing, and Bible literature is needed here in Tecate," the man said. "The location should be just north of the border on the United States side. A mission station is also needed for God's workers traveling south or returning north."

Then the man looked straight at Paul—looked

him right in the eye—and said, "I'm sure you can do it, because you are qualified and called."

The stranger said nothing else, not even good-bye, and left just as suddenly as he had come. Paul sat stunned for a moment and then hurried to the front office where the secretary worked.

"Did you see the stranger who was just here?" he asked.

The secretary looked at Paul in bewilderment. A stranger? No, she hadn't seen anyone. The front door was right in front of her desk. If a man had come in or out, she surely would have seen him. No, she was sure. No one had been there that morning.

The puzzling encounter played over and over in Paul's mind for days. A warehouse?

The puzzling encounter played over and over in Paul's mind for days. A warehouse? No warehouses were available on the California side of the border. There was only dry, empty land, and little of it for sale. What could the stranger have meant? Had he just imagined the entire episode?

Not long afterward, a friend stopped by to see Paul. At least this visitor was someone he knew.

"There's a 12-acre parcel of land available about half a mile from here along the border," said the friend. "Just off the main highway. The owners are older people, retired now. I think they might be ready to sell."

Paul and his friend drove to the site immediately, but there wasn't much to see. Scrubby brush and some wild trees dotted the hilly acreage, typical of the border area's desert backcountry. County records showed the property was landlocked with no entrance from the highway.

The next day Paul asked Tina to come with him to look at the site again. "Are you sure about this?" she asked. "Is this a good place for a warehouse?"

But the question really wasn't whether it was a good site, because in fact it was the only site available. That night Paul called the owners, who lived 50 miles away in El Cajon. Introducing himself, he told the couple about the plans to open a mission station.

"Yes, I know about you and your good work with the mission school," the wife said. "We'd like to sell the property to you, but we can't give it away. Why don't you make an offer?"

The Joneses had no cash on hand, and their house in Montclair was still unsold. They offered to put up a $50 deposit with the promise to escrow another $450. The owners didn't even respond.

Paul and Tina couldn't increase their offer, and Paul's strange visitor hadn't told him how to buy land without money. The Joneses set their dream aside and went back to work at the mission school. Eventually they left the school and opened an office in town.

One year passed and then another. One day, out of the blue, the landowner called. The property still hadn't sold, and they had been thinking about the Joneses. "It doesn't come close to the market value of the land," the woman said, "but we've decided to accept your offer."

Vida Nueva—transformation of the scrubby desert land

Soon after that phone call, a friend stopped in for advice about traveling in Mexico. Paul hadn't seen him for five years. As they visited, Paul told him about the mission station he and Tina hoped to open. As the man rose to leave, he said, "I'd like to make a contribution to your dream," and he wrote a check, laid it on Paul's desk, and started out the door. Then he stopped. Without a word he turned around, picked up the check, crumpled it into a ball, and threw it in the wastebasket. Paul's heart sank; maybe his friend had changed his mind. But the man wrote another check and went on his way.

Paul picked the crumpled check out of the wastebasket and smoothed it out. On the line was written "$50." Then he looked at the second check, still on his desk. The man had indeed changed his mind; the new check was for $500—enough to make good on their offer for the land.

The terms of the contract called for full payment in three years, but Paul and Tina weren't worried. God had sent the stranger, He had sent the land, and He had sent the escrow funds. He surely would send the rest of the money when they needed it.

3
No Time to Waste

Paul and Tina stood once again on a hilltop and surveyed the scrubby desert land they now owned. They agreed immediately about one thing: since they were in their late 50s, they'd better get to work right away!

The access problem turned out to be no problem. The owners of the adjacent frontage property allowed the Joneses a 30-foot easement. But water *was* a problem. They would have to dig a well. But where? And even if they knew where to dig, how would they pay for the work?

Without answers to either question, Paul called a local well-digger who knew how to "witch" for water. After listening to Paul describe the plans for a mission station, he scouted two likely places for a well. The next day Paul was surprised to see drilling equipment and workmen already on the site. "Wait!" he called. "I didn't ask for work to be started here. I don't have the money to pay for this yet."

The foreman shrugged. "All we know is that the boss said to get started."

Apparently God had a payment plan Paul didn't know about.

Paul visited the drilling site each day for several days, and each day he was disappointed. One hundred, two hundred, three hundred feet down the workmen drilled and still no water. One gray, misty day, as he turned away from the still-dry well, Paul looked up and cried out, "O God, we must have water! You gave us this property, and there is no water." As he prayed, the sky cleared over the drilling site and a gusher of clean, clear water burst from the ground, flowing 20 gallons per minute. The well has never run dry.

Paul and Tina ... watched as one miracle followed another.

The well-digger's charges totaled $3,000, but he wrote a note on the bill saying the money was due whenever the Joneses could pay it. Soon after, a member of the Nazarene church in Twentynine Palms, California, a person Paul had met only once, sent a check for $2,750. God's well was not only abundant; it was paid for!

Paul and Tina incorporated the mission as Vida Nueva Compassionate Ministry Center in August 1982 and watched as one miracle followed another. Work and Witness teams, volunteers from Nazarene and other churches, and Mobile Missionary Assistance groups built a two-bedroom house, a warehouse with refrigeration, a multipurpose room with a kitchen and dining room, dormitories, rest rooms and showers, a chapel, a workshop, 10 RV slots, storage buildings, and an office.

And, finally, the Joneses' house in Montclair

sold. The proceeds were just enough to pay off the balance due on the land.

Gloria a Dios!

As Vida Nueva expanded its ministry, it reached out to about 35 ministries along the 1,000-mile Baja California peninsula, from Tecate at the northern border to La Paz in the south. Churches, other missions, and orphanages counted on Vida Nueva for food, clothing, Bibles, and other literature, which they in turn distributed. This ministry, which Paul and Tina called a ministry of helps, remained the heart of Vida Nueva's work for more than 20 years. Ministry centers located just south of the border could come anytime to pick up supplies. About twice a year, trucks and RVs formed a caravan to stock the ministries farther south.

Tina served as president of the board of directors and oversaw the storage and distribution of the food and clothing so vital to the mission's outreach. Usually donations covered the need, but occasionally the cupboard was nearly bare. One such time, Tina went before the Lord in tears. "Forgive me, Lord, for doubting Your promise that You will never leave us," she prayed. "You gave us this ministry, and it's Your work. Send us the provisions we need to carry on."

That same night, the telephone rang. The caller must have been listening to Tina's prayer. "We have a trailer and truckload of food and supplies for your mission," he said. "Can we come tomorrow?" The speaker was an old friend from Bass Lake in northern California. The Joneses had not seen him for many years, yet he was in Tecate on the very day the

Vida Nueva's warehouse

warehouse was nearly empty. "We are only a link in the chain," Tina says, remembering that day. "We receive out of the abundance of God's love, and we give to show how much we care."

That caring bore much fruit in the lives of people the Joneses met along the road as they caravanned from Tecate to La Paz.

4

Looking for God in Tecate

"There's a saying in my town of Torreón," said Señor Refugio Lomeli: "'Mexico is so far from God and so close to the United States of America. If you want to find God, go to the border.'"

Paul could only look in amazement at the man seated across from him at a restaurant in Tecate. Seventy-three years old, Refugio had come more than 2,000 miles with three burros and two covered wagons. His long, gray hair and beard, uncut for more than two years, made him look like a vagabond, but he wasn't an aimless drifter. He knew what he wanted.

"I talked to the *curandero* (a kind of medicine man) in Torreón, but after three visits I was irritated," said Refugio. "He wasn't helping me feel better. 'Look,' the curandero told me, 'I'm doing all I can. I can't make you any younger!' But I told him, 'I don't want to be any younger. I just want to keep growing older!' Señor Paul, I don't want to die at home without God."

Refugio had been traveling from town to town for a long time. His presence always caused a stir, and restaurant owners gladly paid for his meals because curious townspeople would crowd around the wagons wherever he stopped. "To move on is to live and find God," he would say, but in all his years of traveling, he had not found Him. Finally his journey brought him to Tecate.

Paul visited with Refugio over several days, talking with the old man about God, His Son, and salvation. Paul explained that God was alive in Torreón as well as there in Tecate, that He was waiting for Refugio to confess his sins and accept salvation through Jesus Christ.

Paul gave Refugio a Spanish Bible, and a few days later the old man and his wagons and burros were gone. But he was no longer looking for God; in fact, God was traveling with him. At the end of his long, treacherous journey to Tecate, he had found the Savior he had sought for so long.

5

God Redeems a Drunk

Pedro Serrato Valdivia beat his wife after every alcoholic binge, enraged because he could find no more alcohol in the house. In fact, there was usually little of anything to eat in the house, because Pete—so-called because he could speak English—rarely brought his paycheck home.

Today, Pete is a pastor and director emeritus of Seminario Teológico de Baja California, one of the ministries supplied by Vida Nueva and where Paul once taught English.

Pete grew up in Texas, but when World War II started and young men his age were being drafted, his parents moved with him back to Mexico. Pete met and married his wife, Rebecca, and children—Sonja, Yolanda, Sandra, and Pedro Jr.—filled their home in Testerraso. But the heart of Pedro's home was not his family; it was alcohol.

In 1960 Ed Whitford, a missionary from the Advent Christian General Conference, stopped in Testerraso to pass out Bibles and maybe start a church. Rebecca accepted one of the Bibles as well as some food and clothing for her family. Then the missionary gave her the best gift of all; he led her to faith in Jesus Christ. Starved for this Good News, she read her Bible every day and learned to live as a Christian in spite of her husband's binges and violent rages.

Pete would not hear the missionary's talk of Jesus. But one day he needed a ride to Tecate. He intended to pick up a job there and work just long enough to buy more alcohol. When Ed offered to drive him to town, he accepted. Pete, a captive audience during the trip, heard Ed talk about the Lord. Rebecca's faithfulness over the previous six months had begun to work on Pete. This time, for once, he listened.

Throwing a handful of dirt in the air, the men dedicated the land to God.

On the road and afterward, Pete was full of questions. Yes, he had noticed the change in Rebecca. But could someone like him really be new again? Who was this Jesus anyway? How exactly did a person pray? How could he become a Christian?

Pete prayed and prayed, three times daily for several days. Then Ed Whitford led him in the prayer of repentance, and Pete accepted Jesus as his Savior.

"Dios me ha adoptado!" he cried, his eyes shining. "God has adopted me into His family!"

Soon after Pete was saved, he met a Christian from California who owned land near Tecate. As the two walked around the property, they talked about planting a Bible institute and church. Throwing a handful of dirt in the air, the men dedicated the land to God, and over time He provided volunteers and resources to build and operate the school.

The first three-year course of study leading to ordination began in 1964. Two students from the first graduating class, Javier Rodriguez Díaz and Marceleno de la Torre, married Pete's daughters Sandra and Yolanda. Javier later became the school's director, while Marceleno became the first pastor of Iglesia Hermosa (Beautiful Church).

Today the school is fully qualified as a seminary. Beautiful Church, started with 35 members, has grown to more than 400. The church stands atop the hill where Pete, now nearly 80 years old, first threw that handful of dirt in the air.

6

Caravan Stop in San Vicente

As Hagar, pregnant and mistreated, sat beside the spring on the way to Shur with nowhere to go, God saw her. That knowledge alone gave her the courage to return to Sarai and Abram, and she gave God the name *Lahai Roi*—"the One who sees me" (Genesis 16).

God also sees San Vicente, a town 125 miles south of Tecate. About 1,200 people live in San Vicente most of the year, but during harvest the population swells to 4,000 as migrant workers come to labor in the fields. On its twice-yearly run down the Baja California peninsula, the Vida Nueva caravan stopped in San Vicente at La Hai Roi, a mission church and first-aid station serving the desperately needy migrant workers.

La Hai Roi is the dream of Naomi, a young Hispanic woman. She knew God was calling her to His service, but she wasn't ready to say yes and had no idea how she would minister if she did. The daughter of a funeral director from south Los Angeles, she first thought of opening a first-aid clinic in the barrio where she lived. A trip down the highway to San

La Hai Roi mission in San Vicente

Vicente at harvest changed her mind. She began helping the migrant workers who poured into town.

Sonia, a local property owner, quietly watched as Naomi ministered among the migrants. Convinced of Naomi's commitment, Sonia offered her a permanent place to open La Hai Roi. The Vida Nueva caravan always stopped overnight in San Vicente, and after its cargo of food, clothing, and Bibles was safely stored at La Hai Roi, the caravanners shared the gospel with the workers.

As the caravan made its way through San Vicente, it also stopped at Rancho Santa Marta, home for about 60 boys and girls whose learning disabilities keep them out of public schools. The Mexican government established the ranch with the stipulation that other disabled children from the area would also be welcome. The more children, the better, say Bill and Kay, who direct the facility.

The final stop in San Vicente was a Nazarene church led for years by Pastor Mercado. The locals called him "the fisherman" because he often traveled the 12 miles west to the ocean to fish. But he wanted only to be a *pescador de hombres*—"fisher of men."

Naomi, Sonia, Bill and Kay, and Pastor Mercado all are under God's watchful eye. Through the love of these servants and the helping ministry of Vida Nueva, the migrant workers and children, like Hagar, have been able to see the One who also sees them.

7

On the Road to Doña's Town

One of the caravan's farthest stops was El Rosario, way down the Baja California peninsula along a narrow, two-lane highway. Crops of tomatoes, peppers, and other vegetables destined for U.S. markets stretch from both sides of the road. From the windows in their RVs and pickups, the Vida Nueva caravan crew would see whole families of migrant workers bent over crops from early morning to late afternoon. The workers' temporary homes, shabby cardboard shacks roofed with blue tarps, lack even the most modest conveniences. During harvest season, the migrants, mostly Mextico and Oaxaca Indians, push El Rosario's population to more than 150,000.

The highway wasn't even paved in 1969 when the Joneses first drove their Volkswagen over the rutted dirt road into El Rosario. They stopped for breakfast at a restaurant, and the owner herself turned out a feast of lobster and eggs for the American travelers. As they ate, the owner, Doña Anita Grosso de Espinoza, talked about the road. It was going to be paved in the next couple of years, she said, and she was worried. "Bad road bring good people. Good roads will bring all kinds of people to my pueblo town." Then 61 years old, Doña Anita cared for the migrant workers and acted as a kind of mayor, judge, and teacher for "her" town.

Doña, as the Joneses called her, had seen much in her long years. Forced out of El Rosario by the Revolution of 1913, her family traveled by wagon to California when Doña was just five. There she learned to read and write, but the family's heart was back in Mexico, and they returned in 1927. Doña married Heraclio, a ranchero (cowboy), and eventually their family included 10 children.

Her restaurant, Mama Espinoza's, rates a mention in travel guidebooks.

When Paul and Tina first met Doña, she was a faithful member of the town's Catholic mission. Then the young priest ran off with a local señorita, and no other priest came to take his place. Doña stopped going to the church.

The Joneses didn't see her for several years. Then in 1987 they got word that an elderly woman in El Rosario had donated land and started a Nazarene church. She also had started Guayaquil and El Malvar, two outlying missions where Mextico and Oaxaca workers could worship. As they listened to the story, the Joneses were convinced that the woman had to be the same Doña they had met many years before.

Doña tells her own story best in her autobiography, *Reflections:*

When my son returned from [an] internship in El Rosario, he shared his new faith with his father, who also accepted Jesus Christ as [his] personal Lord and Savior. I protested . . . believing this was of the devil. But within the year, I, too, had been convicted by the Holy Spirit of God, and I willingly followed the path of my husband and son.

Then my son Antonio became a Christian. The Lord spared Antonio from liver failure, and he is now a minister in Ensenada. The rest of my family soon followed in accepting the new life in Christ.

As Doña unselfishly served her town, her reputation spread. Her restaurant, Mama Espinoza's,

Doña *(second from left)* with Paul and Tina *(far right)*

rates a mention in travel guidebooks, and even *National Geographic* took note of her, calling her the "gray haired matriarch of El Rosario" in its December 1989 issue. But to Paul and Tina, she is a modern-day saint. They added her home to Vida Nueva's caravan route, and from their warehouse they helped Doña shoulder her burden for El Rosario.

The good road that used to worry Doña has brought good things from Vida Nueva to "her" town. She was still going strong in 2002 at age 94, still serving, still rejoicing in the Lord.

8

Isn't It Time to Retire?

"Why do you do this?" friends asked Paul and Tina Jones as the years passed and the Joneses entered their 60s and then their 70s. "After all, you simply cannot feed and clothe all the destitute people of Baja California." Paul answered their questions when he wrote:

"That may be true—we can't help them all—but we can help some, and that's all that God requires. Will there be eternal rewards? I'm sure there will be, not only for us but also for all who respond to the call, 'Therefore go and make disciples of all nations, baptizing them in the name of the Father and of the Son and of the Holy Spirit, and teaching them to obey everything I have commanded you' (Matthew 28:19-20).

"But do we do what we do for eternal rewards? We find God, we make a commitment, we find joy. We have so much joy that we want to serve God out of our gratitude. Because God is a God of compassion, we express our compassion to our neighbors who are destitute.

"We do what we do also because of the first commandment, to love the Lord with all our heart,

Tina and Paul

soul, and mind, and because of the second commandment, to love our neighbors (Luke 10:27).

"We agree with the people we have met along the road from Tecate to La Paz—Refugio, Pete, Naomi, Sonia, Pastor Mercado, Doña Anita, Bill and Kay, and so many, many more. When I asked Doña about an eternal reward, she said, 'I consider it a blessing to help the migrant workers. This is my joy and my reward. The eternal reward is in the hands of my Father in heaven.'

"Pastor Pete said the same: 'God has adopted me into His family, and I have experienced new life. This is reward enough for me. If there is an eternal reward, then it is only *pan dulce de vida*—the sweet bread of life.'"

Epilogue

Paul Jones claimed his eternal reward on January 12, 2002, at the age of 79. He worked at Vida Nueva right up until the day he suffered a stroke on August 17, 2001. Then cancer, which he had beaten in the early 1990s, came back with a vengeance. By God's mercy, he endured no pain at all until five days before his death. Cremated according to his wishes, his ashes were scattered at the foot of the cross that stands behind the house at Vida Nueva. At the memorial service, the pastor said, "After Paul died, people said to me, 'I had no idea that Paul was 79 years old!' I tell you the truth: Paul himself didn't know he was 79!"

Neither Paul nor Tina ever regretted for a moment the sudden turn their lives took just when they might have expected to settle into comfortable retirement. Paul knew why he continued to study for ordination, which he achieved at the age of 76. In his journal, he quoted from *Catch the Age Wave* by Win and Charles Arn: "We don't retire as Christians. God never excludes us from His call to reach the world just because our hair is gray—or even if we have serious disabilities that limit the extent of our physical activity. The senior years can be a special opportunity for all Christians."

"There is so much to do," Paul wrote in 1999, "and so little time."

❋   ❋   ❋

Tina Jones, now 76, lives in Sun City, California. Drug smuggling has made it dangerous for her to stay alone at the mission. She continues to keep the financial records for Vida Nueva, but she is in the process of selling the mission station to a trucking company, a mission neighbor. The buyer has agreed to let mission organizations store goods in the warehouses and to let groups meet for retreats, but the ministry of helps and the Vida Nueva caravans will not continue unless God calls another to take up the work.

Recently, as Tina looked back over the long years with the Lord and her life's partner, tears crept into her voice. She recalled the miraculous things God had done in the lives of the people she and Paul had met and in their own lives. She remembered times when supplies were low and money even lower, times when she and Paul had no idea what lay ahead of them in Tecate. And she reflected on the still-raw wound of Paul's death.

Then she said, "There's a plaque on my wall here at home, and it sums up what I've learned as we followed God's call instead of retiring: 'The will of God will never lead you where the grace of God cannot keep you.'"

Memo to God's Servants

In his journal, Paul left the following note:

A host of volunteers and supporters have kept the faith and helped Vida Nueva Compassionate Ministry Center complete God's assigned mission of "helps." Only God can recompense them for their devoted faithfulness.

- James Russom, senior pastor, Parkway Hills Church of the Nazarene
- David and Mark Hoffman, pastors, Foothills Christian Fellowship
- William "Bill" Elliot Jr., pastor, and Laurence Reno, Church of the Bible
- Larry Walker, pastor, Bundy Canyon Church and School
- Maurice Hall, superintendent emeritus, Southern California District, Church of the Nazarene
- Larry Wright, superintendent, Southern California District, Church of the Nazarene
- Thomas G. Nees, director, Mission Strategy, USA/Canada Mission/Evangelism Department
- Jerry D. Porter, general superintendent, Church of the Nazarene
- The other directors: Jay Jones, Pauline Read, Richard Miller, and Louise Webb

- Tina Jones, president, Vida Nueva Compassionate Ministry Center
- Last and most important of all, the inspiration of God, Christ our Lord, and the Holy Spirit

Pronunciation Guide

curandero	koo-rahn-DAY-roh
Dios me ha adoptado	dee-OHS may ah ah-dahp-TAH-doh
Doña Anita Grosso de Espinoza	DOHN-yah ah-NEE-tah GROH-soh day ays-pee-NOH-sah
El Cajón	ayl kah-HOHN
El Malvar	ayl mahl-VAHR
El Rosario	ayl roh-SAH-ree-oh
Gloria a Dios	GLOH-ree-ah ah dee-OHS
Guayaquil	gwie-ah-KEEL
Heraclio	ay-RAH-klee-oh
Iglesia Hermosa	ee-GLAY-see-ah ayr-MOH-sah
Javier Rodriguez Díaz	HAH-vee-ayr roh-DREE-gays DEE-ahs
Kittanning	kiht-TAN-ing
La Hai Roi	lah EYE ROY
Marceleno de la Torre	mahr-say-LAY-noh day lah TOH-ray
Mercado	mayr-KAH-doh
Mextico	mays-TEE-koh
Oaxaca	wah-HAH-kah
pan dulce de vida	pahn DOOL-say day VEE-dah
Pedro Serrato Valdivia	PAY-droh say-RAH-toh vahl-DEE-vee-ah
pescador de hombres	pays-kah-DOHR day HOHM-brays

ranchero	rahn-CHAY-roh
San Vicente	sahn vee-SAYN-tay
Seminario Teólogico de Baja	say-mee-NAH-ree-oh tay-oh-LOH-hee-koh day BAH-hah
Señor Refugio Lomeli	SAYN-yorh ray-FOO-jee-oh loh-MAY-lee
Sonja	SOHN-hah
Tecate	tay-KAH-tay
Testerraso	tays-tay-RAH-soh
Torreón	toh-ray-OHN
Vida Nueva	VEE-dah noo-AY-vah